The Divinity of Blue

The Divinity of Blue
A CCLA
Visit to Cuba 2020

Editor
MSc Miguel Ángel Olivé Iglesias

First Edition

www.canadacubaliteraryalliance.org/SandCrabBooks.html

Copyright © 2020 Hidden Brook Press
Copyright © 2020 Author Name

All rights for poems revert to the author. All rights for book, layout and design remain with Hidden Brook Press. No part of this book may be reproduced except by a reviewer who may quote brief passages in a review. The use of any part of this publication reproduced, transmitted in any form or by any means, electronic, mechanical, photocopied, recorded or otherwise stored in a retrieval system without prior written consent of the publisher is an infringement of the copyright law.

The Divinity of Blue: A CCLA Visit to Cuba 2020

Editor – Miguel Ángel Olivé Iglesias
Assistant Editor – Jorge Alberto Pérez Hernández
Proofreading – Miguel Ángel Olivé Iglesias
Translations – Miguel Ángel Olivé Iglesias
         – Jorge Alberto Pérez Hernández
Cover Design – Richard M. Grove
Cover Photograph – Richard M. Grove
Layout and Design – Richard M. Grove

Typeset in Garamond
Printed and bound in USA
Distributed in USA by Ingram,
        in Canada by Hidden Brook Distribution

Library and Archives Canada Cataloguing in Publication

Title: The divinity of blue : the CCLA visit to Cuba, 2020 / editor, (MSc) Miguel Ángel Olivé Iglesias.
Names: Olivé Iglesias, Miguel Ángel, 1965- editor.
Identifiers: Canadiana (print) 20200374214 |
     Canadiana (ebook) 20200375024 |
     ISBN 9781989786185 (softcover) |
     ISBN 9781989786192 (ebook)
Subjects: LCSH: Canadian poetry—21st century. | LCSH: Cuba—Poetry. |
     CSH: Canadian poetry (English)—21st century
Classification: LCC PS8293.1 .D58 2020 | DDC C811/.608097291—dc23

To Friendship and Camaraderie

Table of Contents

A Preface from the Canadian CCLA President – *p. 1*
Editor's Foreword – *p. 5*

Donna Wootton
The Cuban Hug – *p. 8*
Cappuccino – *p. 8*
Rocking Chair Culture – *p. 10*
Cuba Moves – *p. 11*

Katharine Beeman
Motorcycle song – *p. 12*
Cuban Connections – *p. 12*
Tryptych. From the porch – *p. 13*

Alina González Serrano
Cuban Winter – *p. 14*
Take our Word – *p. 15*
Trove – *p. 16*
Farmer Daybreak – *p. 17*
Promise – *p. 18*
Singing to the Wind – *p. 19*
I Have Joys – *p. 20*
For Them – *p. 21*

Wency Rosales
Oh Gibara! – *p. 22*
Moment – *p. 23*
What I did – *p. 24*
Incertitude – *p. 25*
What I loved – *p. 26*
I fell in love – *p. 27*
When the coffee was spilled – *p. 28*
For Sale – *p. 29*
Winter – *p. 30*

I Imagine – *p. 31*
There are Times – *p. 32*

Laurence Hutchman
The Wall – *p. 33*
Listen to the Sea – *p. 34*
Gibara – *p. 35*
Witness Tree in Havana – *p. 36*
The Water Is So Wild This Morning – *p. 37*
Resonance – *p. 38*

Adislenis Castro Ruiz
Path – *p. 40*
Before You – *p. 41*
Gibara Dream – *p. 42*
The Rumba – *p. 44*

Kimberley Grove
For my husband – *p. 45*
Cuba – *p. 45*
First Love – *p. 46*
Our Cemetery – *p. 47*
The Wall – *p. 48*
The Eternal Refugee – *p. 49*
Something Special – *p. 50*
The Mist – *p. 51*

Eva Kolacz
The Bird – *p. 52*
Boat Ride in Gibara – *p. 53*
Chanting Waves – *p. 54*
Perpetual Landscape – *p. 55*
Surrounded by Pale Sky – *p. 56*

Jorge Alberto Pérez Hernández
No Words – *p. 57*
Always Together – *p. 58*
From the Heights of Sadness – *p. 59*
Satisfaction – *p. 60*
Faith – *p. 61*
Gibara Breathes – *p. 62*
Nostalgia – *p. 63*
There were Days – *p. 64*
At Night in Bed – *p. 65*

Miriam Vera Delgado
Do not Stop me – *p. 66*
Even though – *p. 67*
My best friend – *p. 68*
I am – *p. 69*
A Miracle – *p. 70*
Illusion – *p. 70*
The Sea – *p. 70*
Inmensity – *p. 71*
His Truth – *p. 71*
Dreams and Castles – *p. 72*
Temptation – *p. 72*
The Night – *p. 73*
My Island – *p. 74*
Shooting Stars – *p. 76*
Desperate Butterflies – *p. 77*
Thirst – *p. 77*
I´ll Know – *p. 78*

Adonay Pérez Luengo
Funeral – *p. 79*
Shelter – *p. 80*
Nicaro – *p. 80*

When you Sleep – *p. 80*
They Hurt – *p. 81*
Last Loneliness – *p. 81*
Possession – *p. 82*
You Overflow me – *p. 82*
Tojosa – *p. 83*
Thank you – *p. 83*

Antony Di Nardo
Playa Pesquero, Dos – *p. 84*
Currency Exchange – *p. 85*
Gerry and Odysseus – *p. 86*
Gibara-by-the-Sea – *p. 87*
Guantanamera – *p. 88*
Return from Holguin – *p. 89*

Ann Nadin Di Nardo
Gibara – *p. 90*
Earthquake – *p. 90*

Ernesto Galbán Peramo
Memories – *p. 91*
To Say Never – *p. 1*
Guilt – *p. 93*
Unpredictable – *p. 94*
Mother – *p. 95*
The Notion – *p. 96*
The Truth – *p. 97*
Youth – *p. 98*
Old Age – *p. 99*
Identity – *p. 100*

Marianela Rabell López
In Another Garden – *p. 101*
Thursday Afternoon – *p. 102*
Halves or Reply – *p. 103*
Evocation – *p. 104*

Miguel Ángel Olivé Iglesias
bridging – *p. 105*
poetry reading – *p. 106*
inspiration – *p. 107*
night reverie – *p. 108*
At Home with Jorge and Michelle – *p. 109*
Poetry Workshop – *p. 110*
Elaborations on a Picture Tai Showed Us – *p. 111*
Lights on your Skin – *p. 112*
My Amanda – *p. 113*
Rationale – *p. 114*
Wishful dreaming – *p. 115*
From my Window at 4 am – *p. 116*
Gibara – *p. 117*
Food Chain – *p. 118*
Few Like You – *p. 119*
new day – *p. 120*
Stealer – *p. 121*
Bed Time – *p. 121*
Light – *p. 121*
Warmth – *p. 122*
Reasons – *p. 123*

Richard Marvin Grove (Tai)
Sinking – *p. 124*
Michelle's Kitchen – *p. 124*
Over the Cuban Music – *p. 125*
Let's Hope They Never Invent a Time Machine – *p. 126*
The Old Mirador Burro – *p. 126*
Tethered Circumference – *p. 127*

The Cycle of Not Waiting – *p. 128*
Heart of a Lamb – *p. 128*
Begged Its Way In – *p. 129*
Variations: On the Way for Coffee – *p. 130*
Five Foot Fractures – *p. 132*
The Same Sexy Body – *p. 133*
Shaken – *p. 134*
A Trip to Bayamo for Lunch – *p. 135*
Waking Up From a Dream – *p. 136*

Poets' Bios – *p. 138*
About the Editor – *p. 141*

A Preface from the Canadian CCLA President

My dear wife Kim and I have been going to Cuba every year for almost 30 years – the draw – the people. Yes we love the warm deep blue skies, the aqua marine ocean with its lapping sand swept shores, the palm trees, coconuts ready to thud to mother earth but it truly is the people, their generosity of time and spirit. My first instinct is to mention some names of those that we have bonded with but I am afraid of putting names in any exact order but I cannot help to first mention Manuel and Adonay, and Jorge and Michelle, four Cuban gems that have become brothers and sisters in the deepest meaning of those labels. My heart sings when I think of them as dedicated couples, family people and genuine giving beings.

Then years later Miguel, my wingman as I call him, crept under my skin – it was inevitable. I appointed him Cuba CCLA President and then Editor-in-chief of The Ambassador, our CCLA magazine, and now as you can see, his tireless contribution shows up as editor of many of our CCLA books. Without him the CCLA might crumble into history. How can I have a list of Cuban loved ones without hugging my little brother Wency – maybe my first Cuban brother – who continues to show us a dedication and love in so many ways including by showing Kim and me parts of Cuba that we might never have seen – oh and a big hug to your dear wife Yeny from us – such a dear woman.

All I have to do is mention the tiny sea port of La Boca to raise a smile from Wency, Kim and me – what an adventure – so many memories have been built by Wency.

Dear Miriam, it has been a pleasure to walk the path of knowing so much about Cuba and its people with you. You have turned into a fine poet and deserve the title of First CCLA Poet Laureate with Canadian, John B. Lee – the honour is all ours to have you both under our CCLA wing.

And then there is my newest committed friend Adis who has turned into my eBook editor – thank you for your dedication – I remind you that you are the loved of Love – I am with you holding your hand dear friend. The list goes on and on to Manuel Garcia, Ernesto, Marianela, Alina and many more that I might have less frequent contact with but have had the same kind impact on our Cuban visits.

When it comes to sea, sand and palm trees we are all blessed by the beauty of the sea and landscape that we find in Cuba.

**Earth Bound Green
Dips into Eternity of Blue**

On breezeless day
looking north from Gibara
tip of palm frond's draping arch
dips green
through cloudless horizon
into gentle
undulation's blue

I hope you will forgive my indulgence for presenting this next poem here in my preface but I can't help but be proud that Miguel titled the book after the last line of this poem. In some ways it is a simply first person expression of gratitude for the beauty that we see in the flora and fauna of Cuba but on a metaphorical level it is an homage to all of the beauty that we find in Cuba including its people.

They Simmered

I looked up and saw a large
stunning orange flower
in a tree over my head
surrounded by an equally
striking Cuban-blue sky.
I staggered and stopped
to take it in, to recognize
the brilliance of orange,
the divinity of blue.

We hope you enjoy this book and the divinity of blue that you find between the lines. Maybe one day we will put a call out for poems by everyone that has travelled to Cuba with the CCLA group tours. Every year that we travel as a group we bond with delightful Canadian authors that become part of a closely knit CCLA family. It is time that we have a CCLA family reunion at least between the pages if not also on a warm Cuban beach.

Richard M. Grove / Tai

Editor's Foreword

January and February 2020 forged indelible memories for a group of Canadian and Cuban CCLA friends who met in Gibara and Holguín City. The book we are presenting here is one of the results stemming from such wondrous hours we spent together. You will notice that Gibara, that dreamy seaside town north east of Holguín City, is an irresistible muse for many of the poets, and Holguín City is no less.

As an icebreaker, I always start my lessons telling my students it is a pleasure for them to be in the classroom with me. They love the joke. I used it too with my Canadian friends and they were thrilled, but I admit it was mutual: the sense of camaraderie and relaxation we encountered went both ways for days and nights.

The following are my words to the group when I met them in Gibara. In my welcoming "speech" I used lines from their poems and read them while we savored fine food in Las Cuevas home-based restaurant:

Every year a group of CCLAers comes to Cuba to escape their inspiring yet harsh Canadian winter. While this is true, most of them also stand in line at the airports with "passports clutched in one hand, tickets and reservations clenched in other with dreams and hopes of sun, sand and snoozes" (TAI) so they can share with us – their Cuban counterparts – culture, jokes, a meal, a glass of wine perhaps, life, dreams, a healing laugh, a welcoming handshake, a warm hug.

Some are looking forward to meeting in the flesh friends they only know by email; some cannot wait to stretch their legs under Jorge and Michelle's kitchen table; many will find the "cool, green ocean" (TAI) appealing and prompting them to "busily write poetry – and prose! – at the picnic table" (KIM), and then they will "stand back to survey the masterpiece" (KIM).

"Whatever we are" (EVA) and do during these days in Jorge's "house of wonderfully shifting time" (HUTCH), I want you to remember that "some moments are like an epiphany" (DONNA) so please get the most out of your moments in our Cuba and knit poems and stories to take back home and publish with Hidden Brook Press, because "a celebration of lives involves stories" (DONNA).

Let's "perform poems in the place where minds and sounds converge to find what is meant to be found" (EVA). Let's hope your "books become a gate, open to the sounds of this place" (HUTCH). But truly, let's wish that we can "write and write and something will happen!" (TONY) and let's be certain that "poetry comes and goes like a doe and her fawn might show up… on the edge of the words," and your days here will be "days when the muse appears unannounced" (TONY) and "our hearts grow wings!" (TAI)

One encouraging thing we all did during those days was to write poems, motivated by the workshops we attended, the company we kept and the alluring contexts – especially sky and seascapes! The poetry we will be reading in this Cuba 2020 CCLA visit book was mostly crafted during those fabulous days.

We were all impressed in our literary workshops by the haiku-like lines Ann Di Nardo came up with. A professional photographer who insists she is not a poet was able to condense in three lines the vastness of what surrounded her and the sense of solace and peace "in between." Read her piece "Gibara."

Both Canadians and Cubans made it evident in word and deportment how inspired they felt by Gibara´s magic atmosphere, by the unforgettable moments they had in Holguín´s Mayabe Lookout and by their visit to the Holguín University. The poetry that flowed from their hearts accompanies us here now.

The pleasure of the stay and the nostalgia of leave-taking are finely expressed by Richard Grove in his poem "Sinking": "silver moon east into horizon above Gibara hilltop each night lower each night sadly closer to our steel wing departure," while Kimberley Grove confesses her love for Cuba in her "Cuba" and why she is always coming back: "it is the kindness of the Cubans that calls me to return."

The book´s title came to me when I read Tai´s poem "They Simmered": "… surrounded by an equally striking Cuban-blue sky. I staggered and stopped to take it in, to recognize the brilliance of orange, the divinity of blue." Tai´s line sweetly reminded me of a childhood song we chanted in school about the beauties of our country: "I invite you to find… another sky as blue as my sky…" Many poems herein praise our limpid sky. Could there be then a better title?!

Here we are, Canadians and Cubans, in a bond of beauty, poetry, friendship; surrounded by and surrendering to an edifying experience recorded in this book, inspired by the divinity of blue. Take it in…

Donna Wootton

The Cuban Hug

Is it a hug, this tight embrace, not shy but strong?
Clasping?
With every meeting the gift of a hug
binds lasting friendships.
Count the long seconds of body to body contact!
Who gives such hugs?
Outside Cuba?
My son who misses home and family
gives me big bear hugs.
Inside Cuba?
Those who cannot travel outside their country.
The outside world comes to them.

Cappuccino

Go to hotel to connect to WiFi.
Order a cappuccino and pay
un CUC por una hora.
Hook up; catch up.

Waiter behind bar delivers
a perfect cappuccino,
a concentric swirl
decorates the foam.

Next day go to hotel to write.
Order another cappuccino.
Waitress delivers a cup
cinnamon topped foam.

No arte!

Still good to sip and feel
a foam moustache form.
But next day waiter says,
"I remember you," and delivers
cinnamon topped heart-shaped!

Rocking Chair Culture
Gracias, Antony Di Nardo

Sitting on the balcony rocking in a chair
at Ileana's in Gibara
              cooling morning breeze
         earlier a parade of school children
before them a garbage collector his open wagon
pulled by a skinny horse boasting a wooden saddle

Dark wooden rocking chairs in every room peeked at
        through open doors from the street
          some with arm rests   some with wicker seats
             some with wicker backs
           a red metal one for a child

I'm invited   sit   sit   relax
      talk flows easily in both languages
            laughter
        reminiscent of colonial times
        what the Spanish brought

Cuba Moves

clopping of horses, ringing of bicycle bells
      Movement keeps me alert.
      I wait before crossing.

dry drought grass, withered royal palms
      Wavy heat leaves my skin wet.
      Breathless, I feel too heavy.

bone-thin animals, horns on lone bull
      Dark soil stirs my blood.
      I am reminded of butting goats.

a cowboy herds cattle, a rider holds a machete
      This wilderness impresses me.
      I sing their industry.

clay clumps of earth, sugar cane like straw
      The past burdens me.
      I think of slaves singing.

Katharine Beeman

Motorcycle song
        on the road to Gibara

Ow! my ass
ow! my innards
ow! my neck
under such a heavy shell
Come back!
come back!
on your elastic cords
through the pure air

        Cuban Connections

      My neighbor's doorbell
  rings inside my house loudly
    how friendly is that?

Tryptych. From the porch

Sunset in real time

The yellow sky
covering itself
with a grey blanket
turned purple
curled up
and went to sleep.

Gray cat with white belly

Gray cloud passes
below full moon's face
white cat with grey back
skitters over my feet
I wonder.

By solstice gilded

The golden rose
solstice sun
sets over
my grey neighbor
gilding hair and cane
aflame.

Alina González Serrano

Cuban Winter
(In collaboration with Miguel Ángel Olivé Iglesias)
Winter's wild and murderous hordes. Henry Beissel

Wintry wind whistles in tonight
through the blinds
cuts our skin, freezes our blood
laughing at those who say
Cuba has no winter at all.

The electric fans rest, cold too,
silent after working nonstop during
eleven – even eleven and a half months.
We are never satisfied:

We complain our long summers are
extremely hot
and we sigh for winter
then it comes making the blankets
we just bought
seem overly expensive, very filmy

and definitely useless.

Take our Word

(In collaboration with Miguel Ángel Olivé Iglesias)
Gibara soothes our aching… heals our souls… Miguel Ángel Olivé Iglesias

Take our word: Gibara heals.
We have felt its magic touch us all
Cubans and Canadians
sitting around Jorge´s table
in his thatch-roofed, cozy patio
reading poetry
hearing our friends´ voices soar
with their poems
enjoying a cup of black coffee.
Take our word for it,
Gibara breathes sea aroma, peace,
serenity we only feel
when we walk to the shore
hear the wind´s whisper
taste nature as it is, pristine, unique.
Trust us: Gibara heals.

Trove

My husband showed me Gibara.
He taught me about salty scents
and mesmerizing wind caressing body and spirit.
My husband led my hand to
warm sand and lapping water,
an experience we don´t have
back in the hectic city.

Generously,
Gibara opened up to me:
sunset chiseling a fire-red horizon
out of a sizzling sea – nature at its highest.

Alongside, friendly villagers:
Jorge and Michelle
the friendliest of all – human kind at its best.

Farmer Daybreak

Written after a workshop led by Kim and Tai

My farmer parents
live near the river
they get up very early to sip coffee
day after day.
My mother sweeps the yard,
dogs bark, hens bicker because someone
opens the gate
day after day.
It´s Tino today, he is in with our daily bread
for breakfast.
My father finishes the coffee,
goes out to yoke the oxen
says Out to the field, let´s till the land
day after day.
Farmer daybreak at my parents´
day after day.

Promise

My life is a fight
I have every day
inspired
by my granddaughter´s
jingle bell laughter
and my family´s support.
I come and go
cross spaces
struggling against unforgiving time;

all I ask for is love, a hug
and a kiss as silent promise
we will be together,

all of us,
each new dawn.

Singing to the Wind

In times of trouble
I sing to the wind,
my husband smiles and looks at me
he knows something worries me.
Then the sun rises
in our hearts
and bad things go away
leaving room to joy.

In times of trouble
we must sing out loud
and smile;
then all that is bad will leave
our hearts.

I Have Joys

(In collaboration with Miguel Ángel Olivé Iglesias)

I have joys that fill me
like the sea fills the shore here in Gibara,
constant visitors in my heart
that make me count my many blessings
time and time again
as the blessings of this town
that we love. I have joys in my life,
I count them all
and go to where the waves play
and the fish splash
to where I feel the eyes of God
looking after us.

For Them

For them I fight every day
Come and go eager to see them again
After a hard day at work.
For them I get up and stand
Smile and love
During the blessed nights in their company
At home. For them my heart, my muscle
My all: family.

Wency Rosales

Oh Gibara!

Oh Gibara! Dreaming of its passing by lovers,
walking along the sea shore
or strolling down the Malecón,
Gibara with its particular lovey smell,
smell of fresh sea waters,
smell of the feeble seaweeds,
stopped in time with your colonial style homes,
homes of the sweating fishermen
and the beautiful housewives,
lonely streets waiting for another festival,
surrounding woods sheltering the migrant birds and
the empty cold caves letting the sunrays
into the solitude of time,
Oh Gibara! the fly of the albatross catching its prey
in the clear surface of the sea
and still the lovers wetting their feet
under the chilly rocks of the afternoon
Up above the reddish sky the flocks of pigeons
mixed with the kites' dance
in the rhythm of the northern cold breeze.
The darkness of the night lifts its soft veil
and the lovers leave their traces
in the dark sand
not to return with the passing of the time.
Oh Gibara! be my lover so I can
always come back to your arms.

Moment

The keen howling of the street dogs in the distance and the contrast of the sun scratching the horizon, auguring a such an empty moon as the sad farewell you left in the kitchen.
Trying to catch the sound of the whispers, and there were just the remains of the soft spirit over the untidy blankets, like a vague remembrance of a fugitive sex, intoxicating of sweetness the sin of your skin in the exact moment when the sun waved away the moon at dusk.

What I did

I made up a poem,
me who has never been a poet
I added two sugar spoons,
me who never guesses your wishes,
I drew a quiet smile,
me who has never been an artist
I brought a soft melody,
me who has never been a musician
And we danced everywhere,
never minding the muttering,
Then I brought the moon, me,
who has always been afraid of the altitudes,
And I tight you up to my dreams
without making up an excuse.

Incertitude

I have no idea what we missed
in such a huge space,
Or what was exceeded
in the fissure of our pillow,
By the side, you running away
from your past full of grief,
Me, erasing traces
in the folds of your skirt,
You, with anger,
Me, waiting
You, judging,
Me dying,
What we missed?
What was left?
We missed a little bit of patience,
We exceeded too much pride,
We missed a little bit of calm,
And we left too much time
to fix our pillow.

What I loved

I claimed nothing back
But I needed you untidying my blankets
You claimed nothing back but time scared you,
I was not brave enough to cut your wings
But I was upset when you flew away,
How to cut your wings, if what I loved
Was your freedom.

I fell in love

I fell in love with a woman like the rainbow
with the sunrise
Her curly hair, wavy, straight,
Black, mulatto girl, red hair, blond, brunette, white,
With her eyes, coffee like, black, green, blue,
Her smile, soft, shining, dissimulating, loud,
Not so perfect chins, and a pair of dimples
Like closing between parentheses the nose almost,
never perfect,
Her thin body, fat, slim, and her sweet walk,
slow, in a rush,
And her immense wishes to mistake
the tears for the rain,
I fell in love with a woman who mistakes
the sun for the stars
And looking at the sea, she says there are two moons.
I fell in love with a woman who
after making love writes a poem.
I fell in love with you, who do not exist.
Or perhaps you have inhabited my body my entire life.

When the coffee was spilled

Just a bit of sugar, you said. And
Unintentionally coffee was spilled
While the sun was scratching
the slippery shades on the horizon
Your breath being appropriated by the coffee aroma,
Calmly, drawing a trace, dressing up with your skin
Listening to a song by Silvio Rodríguez,
And a weird pause as rare as his "Unicorn."
The intention was to share the solitude,
Join my trousers with the riveting of your skirt,
But you were annoyed because coffee was spilled,
And you just left,
No waiting the breath of my skin over your breasts,
No fitting your skirt, no taking your coat,
Then came the waiter, with one more coffee,
No sugar please, I said.
It might be better.

For Sale

Yesterday when the afternoon was turning
a glowing red and shadows
changed position,
I visited the rooms of that abandoned house,
I walked the years past, and memories passed by
like seasons,
slowly.
My parents' non-existent ghosts
scampered around shaping their silhouettes
in all the corners,
the kitchen was the same and one could feel
the scent of black coffee
my father brewed, and my mother bustling around
for everything to be in order.
I sat on the old couch and stared
carefully at that painting
where a couple forgets about the universe,
and where a butterfly owns
air and roses.
I stopped to think that life is a surprise
at every corner,
and we walk through life not knowing where the end is,
I stayed like that for several minutes until
someone interrupted me
to remind me it was time to leave,
this time forever,
the house was sold.

Winter

It's a solitary morning,
white mist dims the distance,
and a Polar breeze lashes against the trees
moistened by the tears
of the wee hours.
Birds are quiet in their nests
huddling against each other
or looking after their fledglings.
Roses lose their snuggling petals
and afternoon falls.
Sadness envelopes the clouds' shadows,
and here I remain,
waiting for winter to go
to have again the happiness of your steps.

I Imagine

After the cold, dark and solitary death,
There should be an illuminated threshold,
A corridor guided by white angels,
Two enormous golden doors
Where the resurrection of the soul should be decided;
There should be an immense space
that makes you remember love,
That makes you remember the errors,
Human fragility,
The defects that you can correct now,
And that makes you proud of all the good things
You did when you were alive.
After death something wonderful should exist,
Because if not,
Then it doesn't make sense to have lived
So many good things,
It doesn't make sense to have met you.
It doesn't make sense to have loved you so much.

There are Times

Some times during cloudy nights
I feel that I need you,
Some times during rainy days
I daydream about those special moments
that we spent together.
Some times during hot summer days,
I feel the sharp brightness of your eyes,
Some times during cold sunrises
my feelings drown in the silence
of my salty tears,
some times during warm sunsets,
I feel I need to hear the softness of your voice,
and feel your tender hands,
there are times and I don't know why,
I feel I really miss you.

Laurence Hutchman

The Wall
After a photograph of Richard Tai Grove

The wall is not uniform.
It's amazing how flowers grow
from the ground, climbing the wall.

The wall becomes a fresco of night—
a night sky filled with constellations.
Rich in the display of lights—
perhaps they are like the lights of ancestors
(I like the idea of ancestors,
 their spirits shining in the sky)
the image of time recaptured.

It is a camera obscura.

The wall does not stop,
but invites us like a door into our experience.
It is part of the home
which grows beyond itself,
telling us of the inhabitants, their style of life—
all is there.

This wall open words to us that we can cross.
You can't separate this wall from the world.
It is just there.

Listen to the Sea
for Eva

You make me read nature,
as only you can—
how the sea mirrors the waves
on the border of darkness
when the water is darker than the sky
with only a band of blue.
To see the beach in a seismograph of light
and how the waves moving back to the sea
leave a line in the sand—the little hills of music.

Fire and Water, Black Moss Press, 2020

Gibara

It is a bit surreal how the daylight
suddenly begins to diffuse
from the sky and turn from pink to orange.
The streets are so deserted—
the stray dogs take over,
roosters still crow at each other.
Occasionally colourful cars
from the 1950s (lovingly restored),
horses with carriages will pass.

It is so silent, the lamps
lighting up the emptiness.
Some houses have deteriorated facades,
but the original designs still intact.
And yet there is certain serenity,
the sound of the ocean waves,
breaking upon the rocks.

Mothers with children sitting in doorways,
open doors revealing bright interiors
of old colonial furniture, religious icons,
portraits of Castro and Camilo,
some people are watching Cuban newscasts,
Latin American soap operas.
The men speak in relaxed tones,
work late into the night,
repairing furniture with tongs and fire.
And nearby always the sound of Cuban music,
and Europe's "The Final Countdown"
punctuates the night air.

Witness Tree in Havana

It is old as the broken stones of Havana:
old enough to have seen
the invasion of the French fleet,
the sporadic incursion of pirates,
or the sinking of the USS Maine in Havana harbour.
It had observed rich American tourists and
gangsters strolling under the canopy of its leaves.
Fidel Castro and his revolutionary army were passing by
in a jeep to enter the city's boulevard,
fighting his way to the centre of the palace.
It certainly would have seen President Batista
leaving Cuba with 20 million dollars for Santo Domingo.
The tree still stands, austere and gaunt,
guarding the harbour
by the wall of the military station.
Its serpentine roots exposed above ground
anchor the tree in the earth.

The House of Shifting Time, Black Moss Press, 2019

The Water Is So Wild This Morning
for Eva

The water I so wild this morning
when we step from the stairs.
It rushes uncontrollably around us
covering the rocks.

Before the rough coast
I feel your beauty
poised against the sea,
as you raise your arms and full breasts
to dance on the beach through the breaking waves.

Is Venus coming out of her shell?"
You laugh walking toward me.

Fire and Water, Black Moss Press, 2020

Resonance

1

Sometimes all I have to do
is close my eyes
to remember the past.
The sound of the sea,
the way the waves crash on the rocks,
the sky turning dark, the curlews calling out
to each other over the distant white caps,
the moon shining over the North Sea.

I can see my father standing
on the turret with me.
We begin the slow descent,
down to the moat, out the small door
where an old wise man,
the castle keeper stands,
holding in one hand a small red horseshoe,
with the other he draws a small metal ball.
"Watch this ."
The silver ball flies to the horseshoe.
"That's magic."

2

I only have to close my eyes
to hear the power of my thoughts.
I remember early Sunday
standing on the railway crossing with my father,
waiting for the train to Belfast
and feeling a warm mist steaming
through the woody smell of ties,
the oil glowing in blue and purple splotches
mixed with the sea's scent.
The railway tracks curve toward the horizon,
following the shape of hills.

The House of Shifting Time, Black Moss Press, 2019

Adislenis Castro Ruiz

Path

I want you to guide me
with your star,
so I don´t lose my path
and my destiny changes for the better.
I want to warm my soul
In the heat that you give me
then rest
beside your fountain.
I want you to know, love,
that nothing will undo
the wake left behind
by your boat across my sea.

Before You

And I came before you,
tired, faded, dimmed.
And the breeze fondled my hair,
and your waters renewed my spirit.
Then I let your mesmerizing,
stirring magic
captivate me,
charming my body and soul.
And I lingered before you forever,
shining, colorful, alive
and snuggled up in your lap.

Gibara Dream

I am walking down a star labyrinth,
the world at my feet.
The night is long and it envelops me,
making my steps sink
and lose themselves in an endless path.
Coldness freezes my doleful,
tired body.

In the distance,
an infinite prelude
announces the arrival
of an unreachable dawn.
My soul cries
and my thoughts drift off.
From one hand
hangs a heavy load
of fears, hesitation, misfortunes;
from the other,
a light bag of dreams
and renewed illusions.

The road is abrupt,
my feet stumble
and in the permanent darkness
I lift my arms to the sky
demanding to be understood.
My guardian angel appears
clearing the grey sky
and illuminating my steps
with his light.

From afar the organ stops.
In the sky,
stars begin to fade.
Daybreak,
where there was darkness colors bloom.
Rainbow cascades
fall freely from the mountains
like rivers of clean, crystalline water.

Suddenly beaches surface,
the bay,
rivers with meanders and tributaries.
On one side a majestic elevation
rises
like a saddle;
on the other side,
nested at the feet of a hill,
stands restored
a red-tiled-roof town.
In the mangrove,
thousands of crustaceans
flee in panic from the fishermen´s
fishing nets,
and in the trees,
the birds´ chirping
replaces the melodic weeping
of the mute organ.

The town awakens,
Spring flowers blossom
and in my fleeting dream
life starts anew.

The Rumba

African blood in her veins
a woman's white aroma.

Rumba reverberates and resounds
feet dance to its rhythm,
her burning body shakes
and stirs the whole orchard.

Percussion sticks peal and pound
she turns with the swaying rhythm,
curly, rolling hair
her skin soars and shines.

Drums sound and resound
laughter and weeping together.
The suffering black slave
the girl, she dances with him
a mixture of singing and laments
African jargon as well.

Drums pound and sound
rumba... all its way to you.

Kimberley Grove

For my husband

Most men sleep with women
My husband sleeps with earplugs

Cuba

Is it the beauty of the countryside?
The spider-top palms, nature's fireworks
exploding everywhere in the landscape?
Or the rugged faces turning to sweet smiles?
Or maybe it is knowing that the sun is still alive?
No, it is the kindness of the Cubans
that calls me to return.

First Love

I saw it in the movies,
so it must be true -
a recipe for romance.
I stood ever so silent
in my backyard
waiting....
Short tiny breaths,
knees like rubber bands ready to snap
as I tiptoed on my seven-year-old toes
to look through the crack
between our house's red brick wall
and the faded-to-pink playhouse.
I saw him approaching,
a boy with sandbox blonde hair
strolled along the path beside the road
returning from a stressless day at school
Lights, camera, action.
I ran to my father's rock garden
sauntered among the
daffodils, petunias, and tulips
ablaze with colour.
I conjured up my music teacher's voice.
Echoing her vibrato, I sang
a love song I had invented.
I ran to see his reaction, but all I saw
was the back of him, kicking a lone stone
he had found underfoot.
I stared until he was a speck in a cloud of dust.

Our Cemetery

The lion stood stone-faced
guarding the ancient mausoleum.
I was the height of my grandfather's knees.
He lifted me to pet the time-worn head of the beast
while my grandmother spread the patchwork quilt
on the velvety, freshly-mowed green grass
the scent of the shavings still lingering.
I eyed the plumb, moist chicken
that she uncovered from the picnic basket.
A small black jeep stopped beside us.
A stone-faced man yelled, "You can't eat here."
That day I learned that it wasn't our park.

The Wall

The yellow azaleas slip over the wall.
Purple moss drips over the edge.
Red bricks piled high, with
missing mortar coming loose.
How long have the bricks
withstood the aggression?
Is it time for the wall to crumble,
for the world to see the garden, the beauty
that is there and has always been?

The Eternal Refugee

Break, break
O, ancient sea,
Go ahead
Let your waves
Slash and gash
At stones in the sand;
Makes no difference
How much you stumble
And tumble over
The solid cushions
That have broken
From earth's shore;
You cannot venture
Over valley and hill,
You are a refugee
For evermore.

Something Special

There is something special
About differences:
People are different
Depending from which country
They are from
Not just the customs
They have
Not just what their
Tastes are.
People can be different
In their backgrounds:
Who taught them about life
Who taught them how to care
Who instructed them
How to tie their shoes
Or bake pies, be polite.
No one is exactly the same,
Not even twins.
What makes our experiences
So special is that they are different
And we react to them differently
From other people, whether
It's family, friends, neighbours
Or strangers on the street:
They are different which makes
Them something special.

The Mist

The mist hovers over the lake
Weighing heavier with its thickness
Leaving behind an offering,
A comforting quilt of smoke
Over past agonies, past wounds, past scars,
Seeping into the harsh lines
Scraping out the
Cruel childhood memories,
Left in rocks at
The altar of Lake Memphremagog.

Eva Kolacz

The Bird
for Miguel

The bird filled the air with laughter.
Ironic laughter,
concealed by a few high pitched notes of the song.
Why did he do this to us?
Only the other of his kind could answer.

February 3, 2020
Holguin, Cuba

Boat Ride in Gibara

for Jorge

The transcendent skin of the water
is asking me to touch it,
then go deeper, deeper—
where algae struck by sunrays
were waiting, waving their long arms.

A line blue of horizon is leaning toward us.
We're on the boat ride
to see what it has to offer—
having been named as the land of promise
for sailors under Columbus's reign.

But at our feet were just rocks,
some wild flowers and dead fish flying
with open mouth in the bay.

January 30
Gibara, Cuba

Chanting Waves

Unlike the ordinary movement of the sound day before,
the echo was playing music in the air, humming to itself.
The tides start to murmur in response, meditate.
Misty light was crawling over them, before setting out
on the search, for the place to lie down in the midday.

After the storm this morning, seaweed emerged
brownish and drier onto the beach, coil around our feet,
slowing them on the walk,
pleading to be picked up and carried back to the ocean.

February 2020
Gibara, Cuba

Perpetual Landscape

The fog is rising up, blind and sticky.
Wind consumes it slowly.

Soon midnight will invent itself.

Let's drink air on the sight of falling sun
before it will be long gone to the mountain of sorrow,
beyond the timberline of thought.

Thought can be measured.

Someone moved this perpetual landscape
through a matrix
and vanished.

The beach looks confused.

Surrounded by Pale Sky

After a photograph of Richard Tai Grove

The tower watched me from the distance—
its eyes wide open.
I'm standing before the wall. I'm safe.
I can rest, breathing the air coming from the ocean,
and trail the birds fly crossing each others' routes,
in an elliptical pattern.
My eyelids soaking the warm wave of sunshine,
allow memories to come back: self contained and gentle.

I notice yellow flowers cascading over the wall;
it seems that they invite me to make a small bouquet,
then go as quickly as possible through memories,
to offer it to my mother, before she leaves her room.

February 2, 2020

Jorge Alberto Pérez Hernández

No Words

Lovers
Keep
Silent for a long while
Hold their hands
Close their eyes
When they kiss.

Always Together

Do not love me slowly
like a cheap cider that smoulders,
smoke drifting little by little,
you act like a child,
my kisses do not reach you,
you do not let my desires
throb in your heart.
If our love dies, there will be
no other like it in the universe
If the fire goes out
all you will see
are my tears on my pillow.
Your eyes, the deep wells of love
I know, still live in your heart.
I beg of you to walk away
from the grey people who
can steal your colors,
my spirit is a prisoner
in a bone cage, I need
to set it free to be with you
until we die together,
leave with me
even a small part of you
if I die first
to take into eternity this waning love,
I need nothing more.

From the Heights of Sadness

Travelers of heaven
Humble beings now sleeping
In the Celestial Empire
Tender hearts
The terrifying innocence of agony
The scarlet rain of distress
Without smile
Our sorrowful life
Your apparition sores from the crypt
Spread like a bough of tenderness
Across the firmament
In your absence you leave us
Crowned with brokenhearted sadness.

Satisfaction

Who heard the weeping
of the motionless oak trees
up there on the rough mountain
soil
when they were being chopped down?
Who in the coppery afternoons
sought to grant fortitude
to a hundred unfortunate hearts
so they would not fear
a life of peace?
Who led back to shore
bravely and proudly
in the dark November nights
and the sea´s crudeness
the unfastened boats?
It was not only me,
it was God´s hand!

Faith

If you want to fly like an eagle
You cannot run like turkeys
Find your footsteps everyday
Follow your own footsteps faithfully
Your own steps may not cause you torment, nor fear,
If you change your course,
And if you don´t know the new direction,
Be aware of risks, although notably wonderful things
will appear in your sight,
There is a violent universe
That causes fear in you.
Keep going,
Your future is abundant with hope
All you need is to grow in your faith,
But don´t forget....
If you want to fly like an eagle,
You cannot run like turkeys.

Gibara Breathes

Gibara breathes in the ocean waves
Caresses my balding head, capped with salt and sun.
Sometimes I believe, truly, she is a woman
I fell in love with many years ago
Never to let her down
Never to quit her embrace of mangrove
Her kiss of seagulls
Her endless charm.

Nostalgia

I sold my boat, I locked up my fishing gear
I said good-bye to rowing into the thrill
Into the fight for the livelihood
That came from my beloved sea.
But in the starry nights
I look at it, inhale its aroma of coral reefs
And dream I am again on my boat
Out to the dark blue waters
That were my joy, my best pastime
And my whole life.

There were Days
(In collaboration with Miguel Ángel Olivé Iglesias)

There were days of splashing on the beach
Sunbathing until our skins hurt and blistered
But that was fun, and long nights too under the stars
A campfire and guitars
To sing The Beatles´ songs
Or KC and The Sunshine Band´s
Until our throats hurt too and all we could do
Was howl at the moon and look
At the girls out of the corner of our eyes
Come up with stunts to impress them
Half-recite a Neruda poem, "In nights like this…"
And hope they would listen and fall in love
With the poem – with us.

At Night in Bed

(In collaboration with Miguel Ángel Olivé Iglesias)

At night in bed I close my eyes
And feel the rumble of the sea
In my ears. It calls me, sounds coming out
Of seashells, dolphins translating until
They are clear to me.
At night in bed I open my eyes
And the sea is all I see
Dark, deep, dominant
Like stars up in the sky
That shoot down in blazes
And land upon my bedspread
Lighting the room, the house, the town.
At night in bed I dream
And my dreams flicker all night long.

Miriam Vera Delgado
CCLA Poet Laureate Cuba

Do not Stop me

Do not smother my soul
because I still have strength;
to look at that sky,
to count the stars.
Because there is still light
in my bosom;
and wings in my poem!
Do not tie my illusions
that strive to be alien;
since I feel in my soul,
butterflies and fireflies.
do not extinguish the little light
that still shines here,
in my head;
let me dance to the music
that lives by my pain…
Do not stop that being
that inhabits here,
in my cave,
let it go to daylight
and see spring;
flowers, sea, sky,
and the birds;
they will make its life more beautiful.
Let me fly free
without ties and chain;
to be able to find,
the path that awaits for me!

Even though

Even though I don't want
to love you
even though there are five
good reasons telling me
I can't love you
even though I want to
forget you
even though I´m trying
to find someone
that will push you out
of my heart
and take your place...
I love you.

My best friend

My best friend forgot
my phone number and name,
he wrote them on snow
they melted away.
Spring and its blossoms
filled his mind and his
eyes
with music and laughter,
now new friends decide.
Day after day
week after week
I waited here,
I trusted him,
I thought he'd call...
The phone didn't ring.

I am

I am a flowerless garden
Make me bloom!
I am an empty shell
Fill me!
I am a dark star
Light me!
I am a wingless bird
Make me fly!

A Miracle

I need a Miracle...
A bright new Sunrise
of Love
inside my Heart.
May God make it true!

Illusion

My heart,
Mistreated pincushion...
Still dares to be hopeful.

The Sea

Search for the horizon
and you will find the sea...
Infinite, blue, irreverent.

Immensity

A sadness in tricolour
of shadows inhabits me ...
It is the cosmic
immensity
where love flies!

His Truth

I looked into his eyes
deeply, very deeply
and sailed up to
the bottom of his soul...
Hidden there,
crouched in a
corner...
There was his Truth.

Dreams and Castles

I am building
castles
so that my dreams
live in them...
I am building them
with ice, sand
and stardust.
My castles
are as beautiful
as my dreams
but...
Do not touch them!

Temptation

That mischievous brightness
in your eyes,
tells me you've never been
of innocent creation;
an invitation to play
forbidden games,
is always there, in you...
As a temptation.

The Night

The Night,
cosmic mantle
that threshes stars
Enfolds me
in its hallucinated magic.

The Trip

I have started packing.
I will travel with no
destination...
May God guide my steps!

My Island

June arrives
full of Summer.
Summer of the glowing sun
that bathes my Island.
Island that glitters
in all its greenery.
Greenery that mixes
with the beaches.
Beaches that bubble
with so much heart.
Cuban heart
full of happiness.
Happiness that is a mixture
of music and laughter.
Laugh that forgets
so much heat.
Heat of good people,
Cuban heat,
the heat of our sun.
Sun that illuminates
all my Island.
Island that becomes
a great holiday.
Holiday
where we all
sing
the same song.

The song that all
my people dance.
My people dance to
to the rhythm of the bongo.
The bongo of African
Ancestors,
guitars brought
by the Spaniard.
The Spaniards, the Indian,
the African,
a blend that gave to
the Cuban his colour.
Cuban colour
that dresses my
people,
people who dance
son or guaguancó.
Guaguancó
of African rhythms,
son
that sounds Spanish-like.
Spaniard and African
that blend,
gracefulness and charm
that fill the heart.
Heart that pumps
our blood
and moves our hips…
Hips that dance
to the drumming of the drums.

Shooting Stars

Tonight the Universe
is celebrating
Gemini organizes the
dance.
The Stars
in their frenetic dance
glide,
across the cosmic
mantle,
radiant.
Incandescent rain
of Shooting Stars,
jump into a vacuum
full of light,
in a Summersault.

Desperate Butterflies

My hands
desperate butterflies,
clumsily flutter
to the rhythm of an
unbridled heart...
Searching without finding.

Thirst

You gave me a drop
of water
when I was dying of
thirst
my cracked lips longing
for water
my parched throat
asking for rain.
I walk in this infinite
desert
hoping an Oasis will
appear
and satiate my Thirst.

I'll Know

I'll know it's Him
when our eyes
look into each other
and I feel the warmth
of blush
invade my face.
I'll know it's Him
when he talks to me
and I feel my heart
start a race.
I'll know it's Him
when he smiles at me
and I feel adrenaline
rushing through my
veins.
I'll know it's Him
when my body answers
to his touch…
Trembling.
I'll know it's Him
when I see love in
his eyes
and my whole being
will be, with joy…
Quivering.
I'll know it's Him
when he kisses me
and I feel the ancestral
cry
of my body…
calling Him!

Adonay Pérez Luengo

Funeral
(To my Mother)

When they carried you in a gray and almost
broken coffin to the provisory place,
your face the same, pink
like when you are asleep.
We, kept vigil over your eternal dream.
But you were unaware of the gloomy
surroundings of the funeral house
of which we never thought about:
death was never on our mind
and we evaded the subject at our table.

Shelter
(To Pablo Manuel, my little baby)

When this world of subordination
and dependence
is debased more than it usually is,
you appear like the elf in one of your fairy-tales:
now it is you, lulling me in your arms.

Nicaro

In a distant corner where memories linger,
beaches remained forgotten and broken;
sad rusty swings, sway on the breeze.
The sea seems to have lost its memory;
the crowds no longer splash playfully
in its waters, they do not even see it.
Buildings now steal the show
from the houses full of dreams.
Far away Crystal Peak, majestic, eternal,
like the world that you painted for me,
the only salvation in the distance.

When you Sleep

When you sleep you hold on to me not to lose your way.
Then you dream you forgot me,
that I was lost in your nightmarish reality where I am not.
I thank God it is just a dream.

They Hurt

Silences hurt,
the lost unreturning afternoon,
and the empty space on my right.
Uncertainty hurts,
helplessness and the hole in the chest,
the sad nights still to come.

Last Loneliness

When you leave take everything with you,
the hours of sadness, my smile,
my hands´ movement on your navel
and the manhood that grows in you with my breeze.
When your New Moon journey becomes first fruit
of spaces without your shadows on my back,
don´t forget to collect my desires, my caress,
all of the kisses I gave you, and my skirt.

Possession

Body haughty with scientific varnish,
after all its sole wealth.
Spiritual destitution
clad in linen and baroque language,
grimace burdened with filth.
Mephistopheles, passive onlooker,
dwelt temporarily in that body.

You Overflow me

You overflow me upstream,
fertilize my banks.
Your cadence puts life
into withheld lust,
makes it serve me,
fit in my waist.
Every inch my master, you take me.
My hair, curled
around your fingers.
Your face, a virgin of loves.
Your warm kisses,
the desired combination.
Always my sweetheart,
like the first time.
Always my lover,
as if it were the last time.

Tojosa (*)

In the evening, when you arrive,
you bring calmness with you,
all the peace in the universe.
You are a tojosa quiet
and tender, always
coming back home and enjoying
the prison of love walls
we have built.

> (*) Editors' note: Tojosa: grey-colored, white-necked Central American
> bird (Columbigallina paserina) also seen in Cuba. In Cuban popular
> usage it is a term of endearment, chiefly among couples, or for
> addressing children and girls

Thank you

Thank you for burning the ships and coming to port,
being lost is dangerous like the strong wind,
so much wandering without finding you left my soul
lost and sad, intent on canceling the search.
Then your prow appeared in the horizon.

Antony Di Nardo

Playa Pesquero, Dos

Sun, sand, blue sky (you get the picture)
       and the distant calm of the sea.

The mellow reed of a clarinet settles the crowd
       into corners of unnatural silence.

Sun-screened bodies flat on their backs quietly
       seed the beaches with their blankets.

The glistening palms, an airborne succession
       of notes condensed into a familiar song.

On Playa Pesquero the beach belongs to the sea
       like the sea belongs to the waves

And the waves roll in with a song
       the clarinet and the crowd can't ignore.

Currency Exchange

I find the words Patria o Muerte
        and a portrait of Che Guevara
on the same side of a tres pesos coin.

You wouldn't catch me dead
        putting words like that
over the head of another human being.

As I worry the coin between my fingers,
        making neither head nor tail of patriotic realities,
a beggar sits down at the other end

of the bench that I'm on
        and eyes me closely with a penetrating
distrust that I can't shake off.

When I hurry to get up and leave,
        the coin drops out of my hand
and rolls right past his feet.

With the flash of a flip-flop, he stops it
        dead in its track, says "heads I win,"
and pockets the coin with a grin.

Gerry and Odysseus

Every morning, Gerry (that's not his real name),
        raises a stick above his head and stirs the air.
Pigeons come raining down from the heavens
        in a series of pirouettes and spins,
                technical loops
that to me contradict the will of the wind.

I lose myself in these aerial displays,
        and I come to understand
the reach of his stick, the arc of his swing, his purpose
        in caging birds otherwise meant to be free.

Like Odysseus (that's not his real name)
        who bathed in the sea with the sirens
of Middle Earth and was
        unable to deny them their desires,
                Gerry plunges into the air
and one by one takes the pigeons into his hands,
        gently folds their wings
and rescues them from the vast emptiness of the sky.

Gibara-by-the-Sea

Eyes at the back of a head can't see, arms crossed
        won't reach the opposite shore.

The sea, and all that happens in the sea,
      like an uprising from the bottom of a glass,
stirs and splits the waves coming up from the sides,
        radiating out from inside the belly.

Hunger like footprints belongs to all of us.
Where the sands are giving we put down our feet,
      make canvas of air and water for singular thoughts,
eyes falling away from the rocks
            and past the cliffs
    that we don't need to imagine are there.

Above, the sky is a pale blue ink—
you can dip in your pen even when the sun begins to set,
      even when the sea is shaken and breaks,
           and spill a million shards of candescent light.

Guantanamera

I sailed with Columbus on the feast day of José Martí
and came to the shores of Cuba, to a bay dead-centre
in the fold of the map I used to get there by car.

The driver, his nose out of joint, let me off on the shadow-side
of the road and I trimmed the silks in the direction he pointed.
Nothing was far from the truth, he said, as I walked away

towards the bay. The waves were smart and sassy, followed
each other wherever they went, as sure of themselves as I was
here to find that place history found remarkable enough

to mark with an X. I took a few sips of the air, snapped
a few pics and waved to the stars I couldn't yet see.
I thought of the Nina, the Pinta, the Santa Maria, galleons

of such size best left for the books I keep on my shelves.
Whitecaps curled around my tongue as I said their names
and then came rolling closer to shore swollen with the voyage

they'd been on since Columbus set foot on my map.
Here we were the two of us, Columbus and me, stamping
our feet on the shore, making our mark, thinking we've lasted

all this time. And the driver, a Cuban father of three, sitting
in his '57 Dodge waiting for me to return from my journey,
listened to a Spanish tune Columbus had never heard until now.

Return from Holguin

It's impossible to turn a flight of gulls around.
Once they decide where they're going
                they stick to the plan,
     the wheels keep turning.

The greatest poetry remains unwritten—
       we've known that since the very first line.

     Look around you.
How well do you know the familiar?
Deep down in there is an essence that gives
                    a thing its name.

In a song I know, there's a big yellow taxi, big
     wheels turning,
that comes and takes my sweetheart away.

We are comfortable with the workings of the mind
           because we've gotten used to it.
We linger there for as long as we want
            if the words are right.

Isn't that what the poets have always said?
That whether we're coming or going
           we've got to get the words right?

It's a long car ride back from Holguin
     and the wheels keep turning and turning.

Ann Nadin Di Nardo

Gibara

the sea on one side
mountains on the other
and a checkerboard in between

Earthquake

soft, ever so soft
a ripple in the mattress
like the flutter of butterfly wings
announces a sudden crack in the earth
a million miles away

Ernesto Galbán Peramo

Memories

I watch old pictures casually,
trying to organize my mind.
Times gone by haunt me
with flashes of youth, love, past glories.
Promises have been left behind,
there are vague images, and I forgot
the girl in blue, vanished in bygone days.
Dry pressed flowers
in a book, broken words,
a pink handkerchief and a letter
pledging endless love.
Memories still vibrate in my mind
after so many summers.
So much has changed. Time flies!

To Say Never

Never say never; it's quite a risk
better not plan for the future,
not before you are fully aware
our fate is also a part of our world.
To say never prevents the possibility
of making the right decisions:
there is human determination,
divine intervention,
the unknown; be it good or evil.
To say never makes us overlook
those small details, life's perspective
or will lead us to bid farewell forever.
In this world to say never is illogic
for our dreams can come true ...
if they fade, then it is God's will.

Guilt

Guilt attacks our conscience
sneaks inside our minds
in disguise, floods our brain.
It baffles us time and again.
Guilt wears a face, spawns a shadow
when years go by;
grows huge with time turns us suicidal.
And there is no way to eliminate it.
Guilt brings oblivion controls
and harms us with its continuous persistence,
pokes into our sins revives them
whether we committed them
with intent or not. It creates insecurity,
prowls round us like a stalker
in dark places full of names and faces.

Unpredictable

The tree they planted has grown
more branches through the winters,
there will be tough and tender moments for them.
Even if the tree stays in bloom,
in spring it will have what's left
of either joy or sadness.
Like us the tree will endure and last
like us it can also wither.
Life and death come as one entity
they can happen within seconds,
then stroll down the path, hand in hand:
multi-faceted, both unpredictable,
unfazed, to all the hours
we attempt to conquer, to gain ... in vain ...

Mother

A woman I love is aging
but I have never written her a song;
for her it is natural to endure the pain
in her chest, she so often complains about.
She plaits, her grey hair: every single night
rewinds in her mind her entire life;
and when she forgets, she invites me
to help her find her missing brooch.
Time forsakes her, yet she regales me
with her incredible tender charm. She graces
the things she touches. She is my mother
and it is hard for me to put into words
what I will feel when, one of these days,
she departs to meet with my father.

The Notion

Sometimes transparency
in what is said hurts
like a notion told
to others; it is more than innocence.
Absence is misunderstood,
a look, a compliment,
it is a spread torrent
poison-laden too
if the ramifications it brings

The Truth

It hides not just
because up above it is a white
cloud that in alighting snatches
the dark mask. Absent
from what is false, is present
with shaken look,
resounding, moved,
there are those who try to make it evil
and break its wing
like to a wounded dove.

Youth

A challenge in itself
are sprouting and birth,
its path seems a slow
rowing. Madness and absence
of tiredness, inexperience
is what is contained alone,
like a stream comes
from earth the stout spirit
running to the river
that holds the great flow.

Old Age

The body alongside age
leaves behind the breeze
of youth, and a smile
does not grow if in solitude
years are insignificance
passing by like whimpers.
Time goes by, and memories
are hurt in quietness
even if they revel in virtue
they make way to oblivion.

Identity

If in departing you decide
not to look back,
you´ll be bound forever
to things you won´t forget.
Trying to change you ask
the past to stay behind
and leave you like a pariah
with no remembrances. However
if that walk was long
it never unweaves.

Marianela Rabell López

In Another Garden

Again
we have wanted to enter
the "garden of dolphins."
Every attempt has been in vain,
all we have done is mud the water
with the blood in our wounds.
Meanwhile
among psalms
of sirens and a mass
of indifferent algae:
My saltpeter-tasting body
Your sweat
My love, wild and fierce,
The tenderness of your caresses
And an endless desire
To make love with mad surrender.

Thursday Afternoon

Hands,
        legs,
                rain,
your shattered body,
Van Gogh's book resting
on my bare legs.

Everything fits inside this love
as huge as the risk taken.

Halves or Reply

Like Persephone
my life is half Winter
half Spring.
Towards you and with you I flourish.
When I cross the threshold of your door
I walk into the world.
To face it
I hide in the garden
the angel wings I glided with
and wear the harsh-leather shoes.
I walk the streets.
Don´t underestimate this dreamer,
I am not weak, my purse comes with me
filled with wet loves, scents
and songs.
Zeus, why do you punish me?
You know well I don´t want
to be a queen in hell.

Evocation

The afternoon dies in doldrums,
the soul in so much love,
my body in you.
I plunge life in
the infinite everydayness
of these steps...
suddenly... at the bottom of my purse,
almost carelessly left there,
shy, eager, the book
of poems that you gave me.
My heartbeat races,
hands rush onwards,
feelings rejoice.
A butterfly flits about
among words.
The white jasmine cuddles up
to the truest caress.
From out the most tender of verses
a feather comes.
What angel lost
on earth summoned
your plans?
What oyster pretends
to shut your desires away?
Do you really think that with everything
you make me live I could
forget you some day?

Miguel Ángel Olivé Iglesias

bridging
To Pilot Tai from Wingman Miguel

you dig up time
from your tight no-time-window time
gotta run
swamped in heaps of books, layouts
designs, projects
Cuban friends who have old dreams of publishing…

hidden brook press   sandcrab books
are calling reveille,

your eyes weary of
nights in nights out
sleepy sun dozing off on your shoulders
the moon, feeling left out of the banquet of poetry,
emits a silver growl, nips your busy hand

wingman not around
to help you with the
mountains of duty

patience and pleasure prop you up
in bridging valuable
friendship across the ocean

in building
art and lit out of
        tender generosity

poetry reading

... as we read ours and each other's poems. Richard Grove
... in a fragile moment. Kim Grove

as boats sway on the bay
and kids splash in the water
so sway our poems
so splash our words under the Gibara sky
mingling with the clink of beer and lemonade glasses
and joyful sharing

good camaraderie
shelter for the soul
perfectly fragile moment
for my Canadian friends to heal winter memories
or forget about them during a warm I´m-in-Cuba while,
for us Cubans to make-believe
old dreams

fortitude-building moment for
what tomorrow has in store
life´s dark blotches brushed aside
hope wafting

bliss

inspiration

Is it a hug, this tight embrace? Donna Wootton
I write write write. Antony Di Nardo

sunrise embraces tightly
lukewarm water playfully laps my toes
while my fingers
                        write write write
dawn poems
on the sand

night reverie

... lulling me to sleep. Richard Grove

the chilly night hour
sneaks in
to toboggan on Jorge´s wall clock

I hear a shy tick-ticking:
the second hand´s maneuver
to linger on a bi-temporal dimension
while the minute hand snail-paces
from tonight to tomorrow
and the hour hand seems to refuse
to move on,

        in love with that star
        rocked by a growing polyphony of crickets
        lulled by waterfront salty scents and sounds
        charmed by

Tinkerbell, who flutters in to sprinkle hush
Hypnos, who rides a hippocampus...

our Cuban Little Pumpkin (*)
welcomes them with a yawnful smile
as they hold hands to fly over town
raining dreams on sleepy heads;

peace – Gibara peace,
descending upon the seashore, advancing
embracing, blessing
with wings of illusion
all that is human, all that is not...

(*) Author´s note: Little Pumpkin (Calabacita in Spanish) is a well-known TV spot character for children broadcast in Cuba every night at about 8 o´clock, to prompt parents to tuck their little kids in. Its music and lyrics flow on a tender, violin-based rhythm. Written and sung by one of Cuba´s much-loved, top voices, Liuba María Hevia, its creative, dreamy images are highly engaging and significantly educational

At Home with Jorge and Michelle

Written after a workshop led by Kim and Tai

Writers arrive
one by one, faces still sleepy
after the post-lunch nap (Tai loves it)
yet smiling, eager to sit at the "round table"
in Jorge and Michelle's patio,
gentle breeze sneaking in through the
thatched ceiling, scent of marine wood and Cuban food
sounds of pigeons cooing in Juanpi's hands.

They are anxious to pour out their feelings,
write, laugh, unplug themselves
from the hectic rush of their cities.
Jorge and Michelle, the Gibara CCLA hosts,
regale us, first and foremost, affection
then come a guitar, jokes
dishes they prepared
seasoning the food with love
dressing the salad with tenderness
frying the vegetables with passion
opening the bottle with hospitality.

The whole scene is a poem, collective writing,
two nations mix in Spanglish, or Engnish,
superb trays, juicy treat
warmth, the complicity of friendship
beyond walls or blockades or the gloomy threat of that virus.

We feel at home
with Jorge and Michelle.

Poetry Workshop
Written after a workshop led by Kim and Tai

We are in a poetry workshop. CCLA Founding President, Tai,
speaks of pictures and words
and of borrowing from each other
as we share our initial ramblings,
and even my wife is trapped in the magic of words.
We take in the hints, let the lines
unscramble thoughts from our minds
into Jorge and Michelle's long cozy patio table.
Poems are delivered on this table,
hammered and chiseled, then caressed —

Ten-minute break!
Snack coming!

My sheet of paper
looks like a field after battle.
A five-star snack rolls in. We share poetry
and food.

Long live these workshops!

Elaborations on a Picture Tai Showed Us
Written after a workshop led by Kim and Tai

The scent of love whispers its winding meanings
muffled by a speeding car
and sprocket wheels of idling bicycle riders.
She knows she is pregnant,
has come to seek support from him.
The night is cold. Lamplights offer dim consolation
as he, the son-of-a… , rejects fatherhood babbling some
DNA technicality jargon –

Suddenly the night feels arctic
his cologne makes her sick
the streetlights spatter, outraged.

She saunters away.
"I'll give you a ride anywhere" says a bicycle rider.
She smiles and touches her mother belly.
"Thank you. I'll walk. You know, potholes…
I have a lot to think about and do
before my no-father-in-the-picture baby comes."

The blessing of a higher love
silently descends on her
and walks her home, safe.

Lights on your Skin

To my wife, on our 12th anniversary
*   Like honey in the light. David Fraser*
*   A billion stars. David Pratt*
*   I want to burn today with you. Norma West*

When I touch your honey skin
lights flash like fireworks
revealing your contours.

I lose myself in you, you lose yourself in me,
two souls on a fusion course
as the light you give
ripples far beyond our window

igniting a billion stars

My Amanda

To my daughter, on her fifteenth birthday
Always rotating around me. Richard Grove
I scorn to change my state with kings. William Shakespeare

There's nothing in this world
or the next
that compares to
having you.

No temptations, no treasure
no potion, no riches, no ages
will make me give you up
forget what you mean to me.

Always with me
even more when we are apart,
my baby, I love you,
                    Dad.

Rationale

To my daughter, Amanda, on her fifteenth birthday
To light the path of others. Stella Mazur Preda

That's why you came
into my life:
to shine on my road
bring the light
that guides and safeguards
make me complete.

That's why I came
into your life:
so I am spared
from the dark hour
from uncertainty
from nothingness.

Thank you.

Wishful dreaming

My side, warm but wanting. Richard Grove

You pierce me with your eyes
step down your pedestal
come slowly to me
                          soaked in desire

I fantasize
let my mind carry me
all the way to
the four points of your compass. I play

the games you dictate
my word surrenders to you

Freudian, I take a leap of faith... fall into a void

I wake up: there you are
on your pedestal.

From my Window at 4 am
Written after a workshop led by Kim and Tai

Sleepless, I peek out the window
lamp-lit park owned by crickets at this hour
fresh wind filtering in through the blinds.

A stray dog ambles aimlessly by
he howls at the fickle moon
in languages of solitude or hunger or boredom.
I can't tell: I don´t speak dog. Ghost howls echo
piercing the night glass. Coded replies too.

They can't sleep either. 4 am.
The skydome seems closer
to my five-story-building porch. I gaze at the stars
reach out
                and nightdream...

Gibara

Gibara soothes our aching
she spooks nightmares away
and brings the blessing of marine rains upon us.
Gibara heals our flesh, our soul
she sends her majestic ocean to cleanse
ominous darkness, sadness, the incomplete day.
Gibara caresses us with her gentle breeze
or warns us with her awesome hurricane gusts,
but even then she is fascinating. She commands
the ticking of time and the infinite spaces of land and sea
as tiny specks of boats venture into her waters
to return safely home hours later
with their cargo of fish and sacrifice.
Gibara breathes. She sleeps in every home
in every family, God protects us all through her
forever and ever. Amen.

Food Chain

*As tender meat, the weak fall
in the jaws of the strong. Jorge Pérez*

Hard rock is my seat under the night
I assume the ocean
a lapping vastness before me
dark eager canvas waiting for my brush
to give it colors of fish and foam
or fight and freedom.

Warm water seeps through the cracks
I can distinguish vigilante crabs
crawling out of their homes
they stare at me unbiased but alert
their pincers sharp and ready.
They are not willing to wear
their am-lower-in-your-food-chain suits tonight;
just want to roam
stalk creatures lower in their chain.

I apologize with my I-came-to-write-a-poem smile
stand up and leave.

More relaxed pincers wave good-bye.

Few Like You

To Jorge, my chosen family, my third pillar
  Sea of foam. José Martí
   … because I have a good friend. José Martí

Few like you, my friend
To offer heart and home
Few so fond of sea and foam
Few here for me to the end.

Few like you, my brother
To lend their open hand
Few so loyal to waves and sand
Few to teach us to "love each other."

Few like you, my next-of-kin
To make us feel at ease
Few so faithful to salt and breeze
Few such caring "next-of-fin"!

new day

To my wife, getting ready to leave...

small hour silence and chirping of birds
take turns
to say good morning

the small hours defrosting right through
the window
leaving a message of dew, more and more
illegible as the seconds tick by

bird songs travel in the air
translating silence
into joyful greeting shards
and waking signals

a sleepy – picky – woman
slowly dons
skirt   blouse   comfy shoes

loose flowing hair
lingering in front of the mirror
purposes in mind

finally
off to the world
out there

good luck
good day...

Stealer

The first bare trees. James Deahl

fall glides in
baring crowns of trees
leaf stealer

Bed Time

The evening star goes to bed... John Hamley

night bed made
stars doze off in blinks
moon yawning

Light

feller moon
axes the tree bough
it bleeds light

Warmth
With dew… in early dawn. James Deahl

garden dew-beads´ glint
onyx-inlaid daybreak hour
the window´s perspiration
greets me
with
a
vertical
moist
cold
hello

my wife's just-brewed
coffee treat
keeps me warm

Reasons

That's why I write! AmaLuna

I write to keep worthy memories alive, buoying
inside me, nurturing the confines
of my brain and heart;
but I also write to forget mediocrity,
brush gloom aside
along with superfluous moments,
nonsense, emptiness, derision, apathy, hatred.
I write to perpetuate beauty – for the sake
of beauty and more – without, within.
I write to capture memorable instants, make them last
and be known,
the jovial spirit of the human kind, generosity, selflessness;
but I also write to forget vile, selfish, cruel
acts: war for one,
crime for another, and envy, and more.
I write to celebrate life, count our blessings,
rise above obscure times and paint them
in colorful hues;
I also write to erase fear, banish helplessness,
pessimism, sadness, light up darkness
and give out rainbows for free.
I write for me, for her, for him, for them, for us.
All of us. I write, finally,
for you, second person plural
and all-inclusive.

Richard Marvin Grove (Tai)

Sinking

The Cuban heavens
zinged by Jupiter
sinking night by night
now below
growing silver moon
east into horizon
above Gibara hilltop
each night lower
each night sadly closer
to our steel wing departure

Michelle's Kitchen

a flutter of white doves
scour the tile floor
pecking invisible crumbs

Over the Cuban Music

Leonard Cohen is with us
in someone's poem
in the Gibara bay-shore patio bar,
shaded by dancing palms.
Tony's unusually rare, glass beer mug,
presented by Miguel,
a trophy for his well-read poem,
sits in its own pool of sweat,
it is only a moderately hot day.
My lemonade sparkles as we read
ours and each other's poems,
raising our voices above the all-pervasive
ubiquitous Cuban music
filling every crevasse
between bobbing boats,
billowing over lapping shores
and sun shimmered tables.

Let's Hope They Never Invent a Time Machine

They say Columbus landed here in Gibara
or was it there in Bariay?
No, it was here.
No, not here,
not there, here.
No, no, here, no here!
here! here! here!

The Old Mirador Burro

For Jorge and Miguel

Dear Miguel, my Wingman:
It is trying to be a rainy spring day,
here in Ontario, March 03rd.
grey as the underbelly
of the old Mirador burro
that leans into his long hemp tether
contently, slowly chomping
at the weeds and grass in his reach.
Grey as wishing he could have another inch.
Me content with +4oc but grey as wishing
we both had our feet under Jorge's table
sipping on his strong black coffee
just sweet enough, enjoying 22oc.

Tai

Tethered Circumference

A Burro down the hill
tethered to a palm tree
nibbled on a coconut
that fell at his feet.
The coconut scooted away
from him as he nipped, never
getting a fixed toothy grip.
Like a child losing his clutch
on a wet ball,
just too big to hold.
Now an inch out of reach,
rope restraining him
from his coconut frustration,
reaching, reaching, with futility.
Does he suppose
to stretch the rope
one meagre inch to finally reach?
I kicked the coconut ball back
into his tethered circumference
for his nibbling challenge.
I don't know if I did him a favour.

The Cycle of Not Waiting

The Flame Tree, dormant,
like the country,
is not patiently waiting
for spring to arrive
so it can once again bloom
in its cycle of brilliant glory.
There is no waiting.
It simply dangles
its long black jangles,
seed pots for the future,
in the breeze of change,
rattling its song
of hibernation.

Heart of a Lamb

The lion, the antelope,
the bear and the humming bird
sat chatting over morning coffee
under the splendid
palm-thatched roof.
The lion with the heart of a lamb
bleated his way to get
the adoring antelope more coffee.

Begged Its Way In

The morning began
with a narrow sliver of light
that stole past burgundy curtains.
I turned over in refusal.
The inevitability of waking
crept in slowly. A horse cart
clattered past my window.
A motorcycle, a rooster,
a snorting pig squealed.

Without thinking
about my equatorial proximity
and the ocean breeze
that whispered outside my window
I plugged in the kettle
for instant decaf coffee,
coffee whitener from No Frills.
I chopped fresh papaya
slipping it onto a chipped saucer.
The familiar rhythm of salsa
begged its way into my morning
from a passing car.
I am finally awake.

Variations: On the Way for Coffee

Breakfast finished, frying pan toast,
peanut butter and guava marmalade,
I make my way to Jorge's weaving
through horse-cart-clatter streets for coffee,
six sun drenched blocks. Smiling
I nodded a good morning
to a pleasant weathered old lady
sitting on her stoop
selling cups of brilliantly-black beans.
I didn't need beans but I buy beans again.

Half way to Jorge's I stop for a hug from Suzzie,
a happy-go-lucky hair dresser.
For some reason I have known her for years.
Her soft kind face greets me with broken English.
My broken Spanish fills in the gaps.
"Have you seen Momma,
our friend that likes the decaf coffee
I bring from Canada?"
She had an uncanny ability
to know when my coffee was being brewed.
She would show up at Jorge's window
with her toothless smile and ask,
"¿Es hora del café? / Is it coffee time?"

Heat from sunbaked pavement
is starting to rise, dogs
have found their shady spot
for their coiled "It's a dog's life" siesta.
Now too hot to sniff their way
to their next tossed morsel.

I sidetrack
my short journey to Jorge's by two blocks
to gaze, submerge my pink Canadian soul
into calm undulations, caressed by salt breeze.
Sand still clinging to wet feet I call
into the cavernous dark window,
Joorrrgeeee, Miiiichellle.

Five Foot Fractures

Laurence is in the hospital
being pampered and coddled
by five pretty nurses, six doctors,
two x-ray technicians and
an adoring wife. The nurses
were all old girlfriends of Wency
or should I say "previous" girlfriends.
All very pretty and not at all old.
If it were not for the persuasive powers
of the Canadian CCLA president
they most certainly
would have amputated the fractured foot
and given it to Laurence in a plastic bag
with left over rice. In the end all is well.
We celebrated the retention of the foot
with a pinna collate and a lunch
paid for by Eva and Laurence
the great Canadian poets,
both with non-fractured souls.

The Same Sexy Body

I sit in the reception-area bar
with my notebook
scribbling out minutes
from this day's Cuban encounters.
Gusts of wind chill up from the valley
over my fluttering pages.
In the distance a nearly naked woman
greets me, making eye contact she calls,
"I want your body,
I want your body, mi amour."
Singing over and over again
I suck in my ample girth,
proudly I puff out my manly chest,
sagging when the song is over
and the TV tries to sell me a beer
or a car by flashing
the same sexy body
at my vulnerable ego.

Shaken

Toti is a Cuban bird

A flock of Cubans arrived at pools edge
like chattering Toti. A swoosh
of camaraderie flutters
from branch to branch, back and forth
taking over the entire tree
as if invading forces arrived on steel wing.
Children splash with joy of cool plunge.
Shrieking with pleasure, battle over
inflated pool ball. Without settling
the Toti vanish with a expansive flutter.
The tree shaken now quiet,
the Cuban cacophony continues.
More families arrive,
the flock grows bigger, louder, shrinking
to calm only after the Cuban sun
finds its way behind distant palms.

A Trip to Bayamo for Lunch

Gilbert, a handsome young Cuban
with limited English, with his
1948 Chevrolet Stylemaster Coupe
had the miracle of a/c.
This magnífico red and white
USA made dream boat,
designed to seat seven,
mangos pressed into a crate
we squeezed nine one night,
is the restored and polished
phenomenon of engineering with a
Toyota chassis, engine and transmission.
Gilbert and his pride filled coupe
chauffeured us to Bayamo
one day to see some highlights.

We stopped at the gently humming
Town of Cauto Cristo to gaze down
into the emerald waters of Rio de Cauto
to be greeted by our ant-size shadows
waving back at us,
steel-girder bridge vibrating
the soul of Cuba up through our feet.

For lunch we were guided
by our dear little brother Wendy,
el hermano pequeño
to a fine restaurant, La Carreta, overlooking
the Rio Bayamo,
now only a trickle of its former self
serenaded by cinco angeles
while we had lunch.

Waking Up From a Dream After Being In Cuba For a Couple of Weeks Totally Refreshed and Ready To Face The Day

A very fat donkey,
red with a slightly blue ting to his coat,
was about to enter the photograph
with me at the cemetery
on a not so very sad, sunny, cemetery day
but before he did I said,
"First before we click the picture I have to ask,
do you know how to read?
This photograph is only for those that can read
or at least want to learn how to read."
The donkey stood a step back in surprise
at my insulting question and said,
"Ehyor, of course I know how to read.
I can read in English and Spanish
I am no stupid Jack Ass you know."

Poets´ Bios

Katharine Beeman
A Montreal poet involved in international solidarity and with writers and artists encouraging cultural creation as indispensable to understanding and changing the world. In Our America, a dreamer passing, her role is a visionary's, a realist dreaming the impossible. Her work includes publication in revues and anthologies, readings at festivals and other venues.

Adislenis Castro Ruiz
Born in Gibara, Holguín, Cuba, 1972. Mechanical Engineer. Narrator and poet. She is a member of the Canada Cuba Literary Alliance (CCLA) and the Literary Workshops "Armando Leyva Balaguer" and "Manuel Navarro Luna," in Gibara, Cuba. Her work has been published in magazines, newsletters and books. She has won awards and mentions in municipal contests and in Bilbao, Spain, 2016. Her name is included in an e-anthology of eleven Holguín poets edited by CCLA Cuban President Miguel Ángel Olivé Iglesias and published by SandCrab Books in 2020.

Ann Nadin Di Nardo
Canadian professional photographer linked to the Canada Cuba Literary Alliance (CCLA). She has published her work internationally. Her first steps in poetry came as a result of Poetry Workshops carried out in Holguín, Cuba, led by CCLA poets.

Antony Di Nardo
Poet born in Montreal. Professor. Post graduate degree in English from the University of Toronto. Initially a journalist. His work has been translated into French and Italian and has been anthologized in several collections of poetry in Canada and abroad.

Ernesto Galbán Peramo
Born in Gibara, 1965. Galbán is a professor at the University of Holguín, Cuba. He graduated in Art History at the University of Santiago de Cuba in 1988. He finished his Master´s degree at the University of Havana in 2004. He has participated in different literary contests in his home town and received several awards in poetry. He collaborates with the local radio station on art-related themes. He appears systematically in the CCLA publications. His name is included in an e-anthology of eleven Holguín poets edited by CCLA Cuban President Miguel Ángel Olivé Iglesias and published by SandCrab Books in 2020.

Alina González Serrano
Former captain in the Cuban Army. Took an interest in writing poetry in the Gibara CCLA meetings and workshops taught by CCLA President Richard Grove and CCLA Ambassador Patrick Connors. Her poetry has been featured in The Envoy, the CCLA newsletter, and The Ambassador 015, the CCLA magazine. Her name is included in an e-anthology of eleven Holguín poets edited by CCLA Cuban President Miguel Ángel Olivé Iglesias and published by SandCrab Books in 2020.

Kim Grove

She has taught creative writing at Loyalist College, the University of Ciego de Ávila, in Cuba, the Colborne Community Care Centre, and the Trenton Air Force Base. She has been published in the Boston Globe, the Christian Science Monitor, The Globe and Mail, The Toronto Star, Watershed Magazine and other local publications. She was Editor for the Canada Cuba Literary Alliance Member Anthology Sí Cuba. Her stories and poetry have been published in numerous anthologies including Hola Cuba, A Time of Trial, and Grandmother, Mother and Me. She was featured along other three poets in the fourth book of the Bridges Series, Where the Heart Lies, 2018.

Richard M. Grove / Tai

Poet, president, photographer, painter, public Speaker. Along with his visual art, Richard has been writing poetry for many years and has had over a hundred of his poems published. He has been published in over twenty anthologies from around the world. He is an editor and runs a growing publishing company called Hidden Brook Press from which he publishes anthologies and books of every genre for authors around the world. For his poetry he has won a few prizes and honourable mentions. He was an active member of the Canadian Poetry Association for ten years. He is the Founding President (2004) of both the Canada Cuba Literary Alliance (CCLA). He is the Poet Laureate of Brighton Ontario.

Laurence Hutchman

Canadian author. Professor and poet who has published in Canada and abroad. He has received awards and public recognition. He has a PhD and has taught literature in Canadian universities. Recently published The House of Shifting Time with Black Moss Press in 2019. Was published in Tamaracks. Canadian Poetry for the 21st Century, an anthology edited by James Deahl and conceived to offer readers home and abroad a panorama of contemporary Canadian poetry where 113 poets were featured. His poems have been translated into several languages.

Eva Kolacz

Canadian author. Professional artist, contemporary painter, poet who has published and exhibited her work in Canada and Poland, her homeland. She has received many awards and public recognition in both countries. Published her book Whatever We Are with Hidden Brook Press in 2019.

Miguel Ángel Olivé Iglesias

B.Ed., English Major. Graduated from the former Teacher Training College of Holguín. Associate Professor at the Holguín University. Has a Master´s degree. Poet, editor, writer, essayist, translator and proofreader of the CCLA. He publishes in the CCLA publishing formats on many themes. His name is included in an e-anthology of eleven Holguín poets published by SandCrab Books in 2020. He is the e-book´s Editor.

Jorge Alberto Pérez Hernández
Canada Cuba Literary Alliance (CCLA) Ambassador in Gibara, Cuba. He has a Bachelor's Degree in Education, English Major and has published stories and poems in Spanish and English with the CCLA, such as the fourth book of the Bridges Series, Where the Heart Lies. Jorge has edited his own work including three books and publications in the CCLA's newsletter, The Envoy. He is currently The Envoy Editor-in-chief. He writes mostly about the sea, God, events in life and his family. He loves fishing and runs a home-based B&B. His name is included in an e-anthology of eleven Holguín poets edited by CCLA Cuban President Miguel Ángel Olivé Iglesias and published by SandCrab Books in 2020.

Adonay Bárbara Pérez Luengo
Geography professor of Holguín University. Has a Master´s degree and a Ph.D. in Pedagogical Sciences. CCLA VP on the Cuban side, poet, writer, editor, proofreader and translator. She publishes with the CCLA. Her name is included in an e-anthology of eleven Holguín poets edited by CCLA Cuban President Miguel Ángel Olivé Iglesias and published by SandCrab Books in 2020.

Marianela Rabell López
Holguín University professor with a B.Ed. and a Master´s degree. An Associate Professor, she is the Director of the University´s Library, a center involved in offering scientific information and upgrading for faculty and students, and also in numberless co-curricular on-campus activities related to promoting reading, which includes poetry readings and encounters with local and CCLA poets. Her poetry has been featured in the CCLA formats, especially The Envoy, the CCLA´s newsletter.

Wency Rosales
Born in Holguín, 1972. B. Ed., English Major, from the former Teacher Training College of Holguín. CCLA poet, translator and editor. He works as a tour guide. His work has been published in Canada and Cuba in the CCLA formats. His name is included in an e-anthology of eleven Holguín poets edited by CCLA Cuban President Miguel Ángel Olivé Iglesias and published by SandCrab Books in 2020.

Miriam Vera Delgado
Born in Holguín, Cuba. She worked as a Ship Invoice Supervisor for 23 years at Moa port and 10 years as a private English teacher. She started writing stories for adults in the 90s and has received several awards in Cuban literary contests. Her poetry and her short story "Paranormal Phenomena in my Life" appeared in the Stellar Showcase Journal. Early in 2001 her poetry book From the Heart was published by J. Graham Publishing. Her name is included in an e-anthology of eleven Holguín

poets edited by CCLA Cuban President Miguel Ángel Olivé Iglesias and published by SandCrab Books in 2020. She is the Cuban Poet Laureate of the CCLA.

Donna Wootton
Canadian author who has published with Hidden Brook Press. Member of the Canada Cuba Literary Alliance. Her style is based on a graceful depiction of people and places, of circumstances and fate that she delineates in her characters.

About the Editor

Miguel Ángel Olivé Iglesias is The Ambassador Editor-in-Chief and President in Cuba of the Canada Cuba Literary Alliance (CCLA). He does translation, proofreading, reviewing and revision for the CCLA, along with compilation and anthologizing. He is a member of the Mexican Association of Language and Literature Professors, VP of the William Shakespeare Studies Center and member of the Canadian Studies Department of the Holguín University in Cuba.

Born in 1965 in Bayamo, Cuba, he travelled to Holguín City in 1977 for his Junior, Senior High and College studies. Today he is an Associate Professor at the University of Holguín, with a Bachelor's Degree in Education, Major in English, and a Master's Degree in Pedagogical Sciences. He has been teaching for thirty-two years and writing reviews, poems and stories in Spanish and in English.

Miguel has written and published numerous academic papers in Cuba, Mexico, Spain and Canada. So far he has published too more than a hundred poems, four short stories and over thirty-five critical reviews of poetry books and novels in different issues: The Ambassador, official flagship of the CCLA; The Envoy, official newsletter of the CCLA; The Bridges Series Books, published by Hidden Brook Press and Sand-Crab Books; Adelaide Group in New York-Lisbon, and other anthologies by Hidden Brook Press and SandCrab Books and Canadian Stories magazine. He published a review book, In a Fragile Moment: A Landscape of Canadian Poetry (Hidden Brook Press, 2020) and his first full-length solo poetry book (bilingual), Forge of Words (Hidden Brook Press, 2019).

His poetic themes touch upon women, people, life, family, love, nature, and human values. The editor is currently involved in many CCLA projects. SandCrab books published the e-book he edited, These Voices Beating in our Hearts: Poems from the Valley (English-Spanish), where poems and haiku of his also appear together with other ten Holguín poets.

He works in the Teacher Education English Department as a professor of English, English Stylistics and grad courses. He is also Head of the English Language Discipline. He uses his academic papers, essays, stories and poems in class for reading, debating and practicing the language, adding a didactic and formative element to his scientific and literary production. He also does poetry reading in co-curricular on-campus and community activities and is currently involved in many CCLA projects.

www.ingramcontent.com/pod-product-compliance
Lightning Source LLC
Chambersburg PA
CBHW020535080526
44583CB00013B/871